Sacred Lessons

from Wilderness Wandering

Sylvia Dickey Smith

Copyright © 2019 by Sylvia Dickey Smith
Cover design: E. Kusch

Published in the United States by
White Bird Publication, LLC, Texas

ISBN 978-1-63363-400-8
eBook ISBN 978-1-63363-401-5
Library of Congress Control Number 2019941029

Printed in the United States of America

Dedication

My four children, Jim, Jon Mark,
Anissa, and Russell Hogg, have been
with me throughout this journey. Even
when my wilderness made no sense to
them, their love and acceptance
remained steadfast and true. Anyone
who has children knows, our children
are our best teachers. They have and
continue to enrich my life.

INTRODUCTION

I spent the first half of my life allowing other people to define God for me. Many years—decades, even—would pass before I realized I had suppressed, pushed down, and tried valiantly to ignore my own sense of knowing. In the process, I almost lost me. It is unauthentic to pass off as *Truth* experiences, not yours simply because others tell you they are truth.

I did. Until May 6, 1981—the day my dad died, and everything I believed about God died with him. I was forty-one-years-old. Before his death, I allowed everyone else to define *The Sacred* for me. God, Yahweh, the Divine, Mother Nature, Jesus Christ, Buddha—all of the names we use to identify that all-encompassing power outside ourselves, yet at the very heart of everything.

At the time, I didn't recognize the rebirth. Instead, I felt like a fool. All the promises of holy faithfulness I'd shared with others in their time of need now felt like falsehoods. I can still hear my mother on the phone in the other room, talking to those who called to express their sympathy. She recounted to each caller how she held onto Jesus to get through the pain, that she felt Him right there with her. I felt nothing, NOTHING—but heart-ripping pain.

Understand now, I wasn't a novice Christian. I was "the pastor's wife." Had been since seventeen years of age—thirty plus years now—and this God I'd served was nowhere to be found.

My perfect world had fallen away. Like a baby bird inside an eggshell, growing until the exact perfect moment when the shell no longer fit.

When one tiny peck led to another and then another until my neat, tight world shattered. I entered Wilderness. At the time, I assumed wilderness was a place where God wasn't. Years would pass before I realized *Wilderness* is a mighty sacred place. I started over.

This work shares a few lessons I learned while in the midst of finding me. If any of them resonate with you, I'd love to hear from you. My email address is sylsmith78681@yahoo.com

I will do my best to answer each of them. On the other hand, if while on your path of personal discovery, none of my life lessons speak to you, simply let them pass you by.

The book is designed to either be read in sequence, or to experience the delight of synchronicity as you thumb through the pages and choose the theme meant for you at that moment in time. (I am a big believer in synchronicity.)

My journey was, and still is reinforced and multiplied by the journey of many. Nancy Hagman was the first to challenge me to "come to the edge." Early steps in that direction guided me to a shaman named Judi Lechman of New Mexico. Judi guided me through desert places and helped me discover the sacredness of Wilderness, as did Dr. Richard Patterson.

* *Quotes without attribution are mine.*

Sacred Lessons

from Wilderness Wandering

White Bird Publications

The holiest of stories, whether written or spoken, come not from others. They come from deep within me.

Spirit taps me on the shoulder and whispers as softly as a bird gliding on the wind, "You might want to dig a little deeper here."

It behooves me to listen—and dig a little deeper.

Listening can be a sacred experience in itself.

As a white dove, rise above for a view of the whole, seeing black, seeing white, knowing each is the other, and both are the same.

Be ready and eager to clarify yourself. Never hesitate to say... "What I meant was..."

Is it something that needs improving: or does it need changing?

When we try to pick out anything by itself, we find it hitched to everything else in the universe.

~John Muir, 1869

The Change Master is one who knows which pieces of the past to honor and preserve while moving toward a different future, but also one who knows that this is not the same as letting the past define the future.

~Kanter, 1983

Who are you to say that this problem won't ultimately be beneficial to you or someone else?

Make no little plans. They have no
magic to stir your blood. Make big
plans; aim high in hope and work.

~Daniel Burnham

If we are not being effective leaders for the whole person, the whole family, or the whole organization, we need to look at our soul's health.

When, in your life, did you stop singing—lose your voice? You may be able to remember a circumstance or person that made you feel no longer safe to give voice to your own truth.

When did you stop dancing—lose touch with your body—and how did it happen?

When did you stop being enchanted with stories? Stories are the greatest healing and teaching art that we have.

When did you stop being comfortable with the sweet territory of silence—that place where we can connect to mystery—where our individual souls connect to souls of the world?

Through stories we transmit values, ethics, tradition, memories, and identity.

Sylvia Dickey Smith

To retrieve your soul, ask yourself what your favorite stories are, repeat ones you find most healing and comforting and remember which ones you especially like to tell.

Our work deserves to go beyond the tame and out into the wilderness. We must include the spirit in our work. Spirit does not like safe and cozy harbors. It is known to storm the firmament and scale the heavens.

~Matthew Fox,
"Reinvention of Work."

Sight Your Goals. Write your goals. Fight for your goals, and God will light up your life and cause grass to grow on your mountains.

~Robert Schuler

When we refer to God as He OR She, we objectify God.

You have to be willing to stand inside yourself and say, "This is who I am," and don't back down.

~Oprah Winfrey

We have more to fear from that which is inside us than the evil that is in the world.

~Judi Lechman

Sometimes you gotta break some rules to put things straight.

~"Cider House Rules"

When you discover the folly of something you've done, honesty reaches from the inside and tattoos itself across your face.

~"The Big Kahuna"

Creative tension is where I am relative to what I want, against my vision of what I want to be.

~Singer

It is always with excitement that I wake up in the morning wondering what my intuition will toss up to me like gifts from the sea. I work with it. I rely on it. It is my partner.

~Jonas Salk

Sylvia Dickey Smith

You're so concerned about being right,
you fail to see what's good.

~"Rainmaker"

By studying the dark side, we see that "evil" is not an all-powerful, consciously spiteful agency, determined to do us in—rather, evil is imbalance, ignorance, and accident.

What is, is. Write it on the doorpost of your heart.

~Judi Lechman

Every creature is full of God and is a book about God, part of the passion that urges us to create, to display, to tell our story, is the passion of divine revelation itself.

~Meister Eckhart

Sylvia Dickey Smith

Earth's crammed with heaven, and every common bush afire with God, but only she who sees takes off her shoes.

~Elizabeth Barrett Browning
(Adapted)

Let my love, like sunlight, surround you, and yet give you illumined freedom.

There *is* no limit.

Community values, beliefs, and norms must not be restricted by historical interpretation of what is or is not legitimate.

The goal of shadow-work is to integrate the dark side. It cannot be accomplished with a simple method or trick of the mind. Rather it is a complex ongoing struggle that calls for great commitment, vigilance, and the loving support of others who are traveling a similar road.

~Meeting the Shadow

Self-acceptance: To be FOR myself.

Self-acceptance is more primitive than
self-esteem. It is a pre-rational, pre-
moral; an act of self-affirmation,
natural egoism. It is our birthright.

Self-acceptance is my refusal to be in an adversarial relationship with myself. Self-acceptance involves integration of our shame-bound feelings, needs, and wants. Our soul work is to find and remove whatever gets in the way of our being who we are.

~Angeles Arrien

Listen to your heart. No matter how sad—you'll be at peace.

I am not responsible for another person's feelings. However, I am responsible for choosing to be considerate of another's feelings. Not because of who they are, but because of who I am.

Sylvia Dickey Smith

Personal growth comes when we are at
least one step beyond our comfort zone.

Never take personal offense by words or actions of another even though it might be intended as such. Taking offense is a choice. Choose otherwise.

Woman is NOT a derogative word. I am always a woman, but there are times when I simply don't want to be a *Lady* and sit with my knees together.

It is important that I be ruthlessly honest with myself and see my behavior, as it really is, without the shield of self-protection or rationalization.

Very few of us receive the truth, complete, unabridged, and sight blinding because of instantaneous illumination. Most of us learn it one tiny step at the time, and sometimes, even when we've learned it, we find ourselves learning the same lesson all over again, but in an even deeper way.

When I fail to take action, any signpost becomes nothing more than a useless rule of the past. When that happens, the pathway to true change becomes blurred, and I have lost my way.

True change is driven by conflict.
Conflict is the primer of innovation.

Every great mistake has a halfway moment, a split second when it can be recalled and perhaps remedied.

~Pearl S. Buck

Things equal to the same thing are equal to each other.

~Math Theory

My job is not to empower people. It is to participate in the process of sharing knowledge in such a way that people empower themselves.

A person is the world's leading authority on them self.

It is not well to *see* or *hear* everything. Allow many causes of offense to pass you by as though unnoticed.

The point of contact is in the middle—
where the butterfly wings meet.

When you walk into a room loving yourself, knowing you are a creative channel and expressing yourself honestly, everyone in the room can be affected even though they may not know why. As a direct result of your presence, you will see others become more alive and empowered. It is an incredibly exciting and satisfying experience.

~Author Unknown

Pay attention to your *whole* body's reaction to a situation.

Our brain avoids a change in pattern. It requires a "provocative operation" to move it from a provocative statement to a useful idea.

All things and events are vibratory. Vibration consists of opposites— polarities—which may cooperate with each other, or conflict to varying degrees.

Humility is not something you work *at*. Humility is the natural result of *being* authentic, both to your self and to others.

Inspiration offers the ability to be inspired, expanded, and uplifted by events, beauty, and other people.

Challenge offers the energy to deal with events that test us. It gives us an invitation to stretch ourselves, to step beyond the familiar.

Surprise offers the gift of releasing our need to control. It awakens us to the beauty and power of the unexpected.

Love offers the gift of allowing others,
and life, to move us deeply.

Sylvia Dickey Smith

The heart is the bridge between Father
Sky and Mother Nature. In order to stay
in contact with God, we must stay
healthy in our hearts.

Silence is necessary to perceive the truth of our God-selves. We could take the mystery out of mysticism and out of technology if we allowed ourselves to find the time and the silence necessary to access the eternal God-energy within.

Sylvia Dickey Smith

Sometimes it's useful being top-banana
in the Shock Department
                    ~Audrey Hepburn,
                    Breakfast at Tiffany's

The Three I's of Decision Making

INTENT
INTEGRITY
IMPECCABILITY

~Judi Lechman

What is my intent? Is this in accord with my sense of values and morals? Is this the right thing to do?

The original sin is to limit the IS. Don't.
~Richard Bach,
Illusions

Just because someone asks you a question, that does not mean you must answer it.

To ascribe, the intent of another is to "play God."

Admire the wise—of all religions.

When you speak, speak directly from
your soul.

I shift the shape of my experience when
I move out of reactivity into creativity.

Just SAY It!

Be ready and eager to clarify yourself. Never hesitate to say, "What I meant to say was…"

We can never tell even the holiest of stories—it can't become OUR story until we have worked on it within our own self.

"But lately, sometimes I can feel myself starting to come alive again. It's scary, kind of, I don't know if that's even allowed. Maybe you can't expect to keep happiness out of your life forever, any more than trouble."

~Movie: *Before and After*

What measurements do you use, to
know if you are being successful?"

Is it something that needs improving, or does it need changing?

Knowledge not passed through the heart…is language.

~Matthew Fox

When we try to pick out anything by itself, we find it hitched to everything else in the universe.

~John Muir, 1869

The Change Master is one who knows which piece of the past to honor and preserve while moving toward a different future, but also one who knows that this is not the same as letting the past define the future.

~Kanter, 1983

Who are you to say that this problem
won't ultimately be beneficial to you or
someone else?

Make no little plans. They have no
magic to stir your blood. Make big
plans, aim high in hope and work.

~Daniel Burnham

If we are not being effective leaders for
the whole person, the whole family, or
the whole organization, we need to look
at our soul's health.

When, in your life, did you stop
singing—lose your voice? You may be
able to remember a circumstance, or
person that made you feel no longer
safe to give voice to your own truth.

When did you stop dancing—lose touch with your body—and how did it happen?

When did you stop being enchanted with stories? Stories are the greatest healing and teaching art that we have.

Through stories we transmit values, ethics, tradition, memories, and identity.

To retrieve your soul, ask yourself what your favorite stories are, repeat the ones you find most healing and comforting. Remember which ones you especially like to tell.

When did you stop being comfortable with the sweet territory of silence—that place where we can connect to *mystery*—where our individual souls connect to souls of the world?

Self-acceptance—to be FOR myself.

Self-acceptance is more primitive than self-esteem. It is pre-rational, pre-moral, an act of self-affirmation, natural egoism. It is our birthright.

Self-acceptance is my refusal to be in an adversarial relationship with myself.

Self-acceptance involves integration of our shame-based feelings, needs, and wants.

Our soul work is to find and remove whatever gets in the way of our being who we are.

~Angles Arrien

Listen to your heart. No matter how sad—you'll be at peace.

~Sharon Haddad

No matter who I interact with, I still have me.

~Nancy Hagman

No man chooses evil because it is evil—they only mistake it for happiness.

~Mary Wollstonecraft

Old urges will continue to arise, perhaps for years. Urges do not matter; actions do.

~Peaceful Warrior

As soon as you trust yourself, you will know how to live.

~Van Goethe

We are mirrors of each other. What you fear in someone else is the power you have in yourself.

I am not responsible for another person's feelings. However, I am responsible for choosing to be considerate of another's feelings. Not because of who they are, but because of who I am.

How easily we mistake attention for love. Even more easily, we trick ourselves into thinking our ability to control someone signifies love, especially theirs, for us.

~Joanna Field

Love is something far different from either attention or control.

~Joanna Field

Sylvia Dickey Smith

Love is placing another's personal needs above our own, without regret.

~Joanna Field

Love is selfless, yet it exhilarates the self. Giving love softens our edges, completes us, and connects us to the people with whom we are fulfilling our destinies.

~Joanna Field

Love is not getting but giving. It is sacrifice. And sacrifice is glorious.

~Joanna Field

Personal growth comes when we are at least one step beyond our comfort zone.

When we experience the sexual act as a
spiritual process, we reach the height of
'oneness,' of *heaven*. When we
experience the sexual act in an abusive
experience, it is the most invasive depth
of 'nothingness,' of hell.

Upset and conflict comes from: unfulfilled expectations; undelivered communication; and unclear intentions.

"Drive them from our shores! They're not like you and me, which means they must be evil! We must sound the drums of war!"

~*Ratcliffe: Pocahontas Soundtrack*

(i.e., Anything or anyone different than us, we tend to see as evil or don't trust them.)

Previewed responses are what keep you
in your heart.

~Nancy Hagman

As White Dove, to rise above for a view of the Whole. Seeing black, seeing white, knowing each is the other, and both are the same.

Practice *really* listening.

Every child's birthright is to come into this world loved.

Praise Loudly, Blame Softly.

~Catherine of Russia

The truth does not make you free. Facts do not change attitudes.

~Stephen Kopp

What any good teacher knows that a student might not. There is no master, and there is no student. We are all fellow travelers.

No explanations necessary. Just BE.

~Dr. Richard Patterson

And it took all that time just to find your self; and that's how long it had to take; and it was well worth every moment.

~Paul Williams

The center is everywhere.

~Friedrich Nietzsche

Nothing determines who we will become so much as those things we choose to ignore.

~Sander McNab

Every person, all the events of your life,
are there because you have drawn them
there. What you choose to do with them
is up to you.

~Richard Bach

RULES FOR LIVING:

Show Up, Pay Attention, Tell The
Truth, Don't Be attached to the results.

~Angeles Arrien

Sylvia Dickey Smith

Don't push the river. We waste our energy when we attempt to control those things over which we have no power.

Trust the Process

As above…so below.

Refuse to have anything to do with anything (like a nation or person or corporation) that seeks to grow wealthier rather than healthier, larger rather than truer. Do nothing to contribute to that cancerous growth. Isolate it. Let it die.

~Paul Williams

Two people do not have to agree on what's right to be together. They just have to want to be together. If that sounds simple, try it sometimes.

~Paul Williams

Consciously choose, and then practice, staying out of the middle of any two other people's relationships.

Life is too serious to ever be taken
seriously.

Never take anything anyone says
personally, even if it is intended to be.

Always be on the lookout for opportunities to laugh.

Always end love-making with a delightful laugh.

Play together (i.e., spar) with your partner when you're disagreeing. Disagreements can then be fun ways to "clear the air."

Life is too short to stay angry. So get over it.

Say what you have to say and then let it go.

Teach yourself to be aware of how you touch people with your communication. If you were on the other end of your words, how would those words make YOU feel?

Teach yourself to be aware of the expression in your eyes. We communicate a lot that way, often without even realizing it.

No matter how afraid I was, once I started on the *sacred pathway of wilderness wandering,* I had no choice. I *had* to keep moving forward. I knew, without a shadow of a doubt, if I let fear turn me back, *I* would cease to exist.

When you can't understand what another person is saying, don't try harder. Be silent, and then listen with that deeper part of yourself.

Check out your understanding of what another person is saying. Practice honestly and sincerely asking, "Do you mean…?" If you get a "No," try again. Keep going until you get a "Yes."

I always thought that *wilderness* was *where God wasn't.* It took me a long time to learn that *wilderness* is a very sacred place.

No matter how much training you've had, sooner or later, you have to play your own game.

Name it. Claim it!

There is a silent bell of inner knowing that dongs loudly at the core of our being. Yet we charge right over it, not even recognizing it anymore. We must go back and begin to honor our own sense of knowing.

What is actually happening is far more important than what might be happening but isn't.

Your truth is not necessarily *the* truth…amazing, when you stop to think about it, isn't it?

We make three major assumptions when we communicate:

That we know what the other person is thinking.

That the other person knows what we are thinking.

That *similar* is the *same.*

When I push myself, test myself, that's when I'm happiest. That's when the rewards are the greatest.

~Sissy Spacek

I do not think that I could ever really love a woman who had not, at one time or another, been up on a broomstick.

~Isak Dinesen

I want to be there when you become a butterfly and ride on your back.

I feel weakness to know strength.

I experience emptiness to recognize creativity.

By experiencing pain, I recognize wellness.

Darkness teaches me the power of light.

Experiencing fear guides me into courage.

Feeling helpless, I discover hope.

Through loneliness, comes solitude.

The path through despair leads to true service to others.

Through surrender, I experience fulfillment.

I can only know the truth after I know
MY TRUTH.

For me to know *my* truth, I must develop the ability to listen to that strong intuitive sense of knowing deep inside my being.

When I know *my* truth, I am able to set boundaries and limits for myself; hold other people accountable for their behavior; and speak out against injustice and judgment.

As I learn to set boundaries, hold other people accountable, and speak out against injustice and judgment, I discover fearlessness, confidence, and self-esteem.

As I discover fearlessness, confidence, and self-esteem, I learn to: Listen to my truth, honor it, give it space, and respect.

Truth clears away the darkness and I feel it traveling up and down my spine.

The truth of others may appear different
than my truth does to me.

Sylvia Dickey Smith

When in a relationship with another
person, I can trust that if an action or
decision is right for me, it is also right
for the other person.

On the flip side, when I am in a relationship with another person, any decision or action that is not right for me, is also not right for the other person. God just doesn't work that way.

To know what is right for me requires
that I work with impeccability,
integrity, and with a deep sense of self-
knowing.

On the continuum of light and shadow, black and white, right and wrong, there is truth, not only on the ends, but at each point in between.

To clearly speak my truth, I must:

Look at the very root of my being, that point of passion that generates my truth.

Discover where I have been wounded and heal that part of me.

Tap into my gut. It gives me a clear, direct connection to my truth.

When I have completed the first three, I can accept unconditional love, even when their truth seems different than mine. (continued)

When it is time for me to speak my truth, I must go down to that root of my being and work upwards. As my truth travels up and out, I speak it clearly. The result is compassion for others: it is easier for me to sidestep put-downs and insinuations, knowing they are about the speaker, not about me. (continued)

As I speak my truth clearly, unattached
to the outcome, describing it much as I
would a weather report, a clearing
comes, a deep insight into me, and I feel
like shouting YES! (continued)

When I use the previous tools to discover and speak my truth, I connect with that higher power that opens the pathway to TRUTH.

The answer I'm looking for is right there before my eyes. When I think I don't see it, what I *don't see* is the polar end of what I seek.

When you make the decision to trust perfect timing, you have to trust it, even when it doesn't make sense.

Stay Unattached To The Outcome.

Open yourself to the cosmos—grow beyond your limitations and fears.

The butterfly emerges into the beautiful creature she is. She doesn't tempt people to be attracted to her. She simply emerges and glows, unattached to the outcome. She lives. Solitude is very much a part of her life.

I deny my truth when I hurry back into my corner and hide when someone else thinks I am wrong.

To be whole, we must embrace both sides of ourselves, both light and shadow. When we only embrace half, we cannot know the whole, and if not the whole, we cannot know the half. Instead, we see the half as a whole, thereby negating the essence of being.

Before we can begin to know who we are, to define ourselves, we must first give a firm NO to that which we do not want.

Only after learning to say NO easily, can we give a resounding YES to that which we do want. Now we are on the road to really knowing who we are.

When you feel defensive about something someone has said, STOP. Do not defend your position. Instead, ask a question (a sincere question), for example, "I'm confused, help me understand what you meant."

And then listen, really listen, without thought about what you plan to say afterward.

Each of us wants to be heard, truly heard. It doesn't matter whether the other person agrees with us or not, as long as we feel understood.

When we only defend our position, we
lose an opportunity to truly understand
the other person.

To really know who you are, do this simple exercise. Make three lists and make them as long as possible. Really push yourself on this:

What I Stand For

What I don't stand for

What I WON'T stand for (and yes, there is a difference between #2 and #3)

Come to the edge, she said.

They said we are afraid.

Come to the edge, she said.

They said it is too high.

Come to the EDGE, she said.

They came.

She PUSHED them.

And they FLEW!

~Adapted Rumi poem

To learn about a belief other than mine, it is important that I learn it from someone within that belief system, not from someone who disagrees with it. Otherwise, the information will be tainted, impure.

It's been difficult to learn who I am, but it's been even more difficult to learn what to do with what I've learned.

Patriarchy is damaging to both men and women alike.

We tend to think of erosion as something negative and destructive, but it isn't, not always. Consider the *healing power* of erosion.

The end never justifies the means if the
means are not infused with integrity.

~Danaan Parry

The Three Sacred I's—touchstones to guide our actions.

Intent. Integrity & Impeccability

It is not the external product that matters, it's the quality of the energy that made it.

Fight or Flight works well for us when in physical danger, but not in the midst of personal conflict. This requires that we be 100% present.

Marriage is like a rubber band. A healthy amount of tension on it makes it much more satisfying.

WOMAN is not a derogative word. I am always a woman, but there are times when I just don't want to be a LADY and sit with my knees together.

It is important that I be ruthlessly honest with myself and see myself, and my behavior, as it really is, without the shield of self-protection or rationalization.

Very few of us receive the truth, complete and unabridged and sight blinding because of instantaneous illumination. Most of us learn it one tiny step at the time, and sometimes, even when we've learned it, we find ourselves learning the same lesson all over again, but in an even deeper way.

When we clutch a person to us tightly or force our will on a situation, we eliminate the opportunity for something beneficial to happen.

It is okay for me to be noisy, to express myself joyously and with freedom.

Sylvia Dickey Smith

I easily speak up for myself and ensure opportunities to express my creativity.

I am ready, willing, and able to change.

It is my obligation to be true to myself.
If I am not, I am unauthentic—a fake.

Any decision we make is made on a continuum—and at any fixed point on that continuum. That is about the best we can do.

When something happens that causes me pain, and I don't (won't) grow beyond it, then every time becomes "that time."

Naming an idea or a concept does not give me the right to dismiss it as if it doesn't count, or as if I am better than it is.

Sylvia Dickey Smith

The essential questions have no answers. You are my question, and I am yours—and then there is dialogue.

~Elie Wiesel

210

The moment we have answers, there is no dialogue.

~Elie Wiesel

Questions unite people; answers divide them. So why have answers when we can live without them?

~Elie Wiesel

I have no doubt that questions have their own magic, their own charm, their own immortality.

~Elie Wiesel

I have no doubt that faith is only pure when it does not negate the faith of another.

~Elie Wiesel

I have no doubt that evil can be fought,
and that indifference is no option.

~Elie Wiesel

Sylvia Dickey Smith

I have no doubt that fanaticism is dangerous.

~Elie Wiesel

Of all the books in the world on life, I have no doubt that the life of one person weighs more than them all.

~Elie Wiesel

Talk more about ideas and concepts than about other people.

Listening can be a sacred experience in and of itself.

When in a group of people and the room grows silent, sit quietly and observe who speaks first. Who is the one most uncomfortable with silence?

Listen to hear, not to respond.

Note to Reader

Thank you for reading of my sacred wilderness—what I've learned to call *Thin Places*. Activities, insight, or locations that lead me to feel like I have risen above the commonplace, the ordinary.

Where I feel connected to something outside myself, greater than me, and also, very much me.

These are sacred, spiritual places, even when I do not recognize them as such.

Thin Places can even come in the midst of grief, loss, or personal difficulties. They are invaluable, for there we find resilience, courage, and strength to carry on. Would love to hear from you about your Thin Places.

sylsmith78681@yahoo.com.

www.ingramcontent.com/pod-product-compliance
Lightning Source LLC
Chambersburg PA
CBHW070923030426
42336CB00014BA/2516